THE INSTINCT IN BUSINESS

Prepare your way to financial freedom

THE ENTERPRISING WOMAN TODAY

Lucía Dawson

"This book is for you, and only for you. I hope you enjoy it and it will help you along the way".

Lucía Dawson

THE INSTINCT IN BUSINESS

Prepare your way to financial freedom

1.Introduction.

"Don't be afraid to leave something good to go for something better."

John D. Rockefeller.

In today's fast-changing global business world, making the right decisions is critical. But what are the ways and strategies to make meaningful decisions?

Many senior managers in large companies, recognize the benefits of intuitive decision making. According to recent studies, it is better to rely on visceral instinct than rational

thinking in many business situations. This is justified, among other things, by the need to make quick decisions in the business world. *(Sadler-Smith E. y Shefy E. (2005): Intuition in strategic decision making. In: Academy of Management Perspectives, Vol. 19, No. 1)*

Successful managers recognize that, the time they have available, is a scarce resource. Therefore, in many temporary situations it is imperative to rely on instinct. In this Business Coaching article, I will explore in depth the importance and peculiarities of bowel decision making, its advantages and disadvantages, and finally its importance to financial success.

In sport, as in life, well-managed teamwork often leads irremediably to success. Team sports such as football, rugby, basketball or handball, to name but a few, need a well-prepared coach who knows how to study his or her team's options against the opponent. The coach knows the skills of each of his players, the position in which they perform best, the experience in competition, also their weaknesses, the character to develop the objective correctly.

The trainer, regardless of the training acquired for his responsibility, must also be a psychologist, because he doesn't work with machines, but with people, and these people will one day be better, and another will not be so. One of his main missions is to know how to deal with all these factors, in order to get a 100% performance of all his pupils. Then, of course, depending on the raw material he has, he will be able to propose one strategy or another, some tactics in one game and others in the next, combining the state of his players and the potential and weaknesses of the opponent to beat.

That's exactly what we call coaching in the business world. All large companies today have their own coaching

team, and more and more small companies that cannot afford the luxury of having a coach or coaching team on their staff, hire coaching services on time to improve the performance of their employees in very specific tasks where performance or results are not what is expected.

The figure of the Coach within the company represents the person who will squeeze all your skills, will correct your defects so that you improve in the weakest aspects, and will motivate you continuously so that you do not lower your guard, that you yourself are the first to be satisfied with your work and ask for more and more. The Coach will be in contact with the objective supervisors, and they will draw together the best work strategy, also mediating between them, so that the project runs as harmoniously as possible.

This small introduction is necessary for the points that we are going to develop next. To have clear the concept of Coach and of Coaching that we are going to apply in this book is going to be fundamental to obtain the success, to draw all the aspects that we are going to try to promote in a firm, safe and irreversible way.

2. Instinct as a guide to financial success.

"Success is doing, not getting. It is to try, not to succeed. Success is a personal standard, it is reaching the highest in us, becoming everything that we can be. If we give our best, we are successful.

Zig Ziglar.

Once you know the meaning of Coach, what coaching is, let's apply it to our main objective, that will lead us, little by little, to the final objective. Our main objective is that you become your own coach.

Now you can ask yourself, how am I going to be my own Coach, if we have just seen that the mission of the Coach is to help a second, or a third person. If I'm not doing my job well, if I'm not accomplishing my goal, to be financially free, I'm going to need a Coach to help me. How am I going to be my own

coach? We have the answer to all those questions: developing your instinct.

Most of the times we don't stop to think about why we make some decisions; in fact, we don't even think about making many of them. We simply follow our instincts. Following your instinct will lead you to make, at times, right  decisions, at other times wrong decisions, and generally, when the decisions we have made are wrong, we wonder why we have made them, why we didn't think of them before, even if there was something inside us that incited us to say: don't do it!!!

flect a little bit, and you will realize that you may have experienced this situation many times, more than you would like. You may also notice that, most of those decisions, have been economic in nature, so you find yourself in a vicious circle from which you want to escape. I do a job that I don't like because I have to pay the mortgage at the end of the month, a mortgage I took out because I bought an apartment for double the price I would now pay, a mortgage that overwhelms me. Now I can't leave that job, I need it to pay. I have a profession that I don't like because I was forced to study a career that was recommended to me at school, I was going to give myself a good salary and a respectable degree, but it turns out that it's not that good, I don't earn that much, and I'm not happy.

You have instinct, but you also need to work on it. It is not all about letting go or meditating for a long time on each of the decisions we make. Sometimes you need to think fast, resolve even faster, because there are opportunities that go away in a matter of seconds, if you don't act at the right time. You're going to need your instinct, that instantaneous inner force that whispers to you whether you do it or not. Therefore, it is vital to have our instinct developed, to train that function of our brain to make the right decision at the right time.

The next doubt that can assault us is whether an instantaneous answer, so visceral, can be trained. The answer is again: yes, of course you can. To begin our training, we are going to adjust to a series of necessary factors on which we must to focus, our strengths and our weaknesses. Our strengths will be enhanced, and our weaknesses will be developed as much as we can so that if we can't make them strong, they won't hurt us either.

"If life didn't give you at least one person who doesn't want you to make it, then half of us would lose the motivation to climb the cliff just to prove them wrong."

Shannon L. Alder.

3. The development of instinct. Factors to work with.

3.1. Aptitude.

Aptitude is the ability we each have, to develop a function, either physical or psychological. It is the set of all our abilities. There is a very effective exercise that will help us to know our innate aptitudes. In a notebook, we're going to write down all the things we're good at, which is simple, from changing a light bulb to translating a Latin text. We do not all have the same aptitudes, and no aptitude is better or worse than another. We will apply this exercise to get to know each other better, and then to  be able to apply those aptitudes to our final objective, which is to obtain an economic benefit that allows us to be free.

There are several categories into which, in terms of coaching, we can divide our skills.

Physical Aptitudes. To enjoy a good physique and that it is easy for us to make effort tasks.

Intellectual Aptitudes. You have a capacity for learning.

Interpersonal Aptitudes. With these skills, your ability to socialize is very good.

Linguistic Aptitudes. When you are capable to learn languages, to express yourself and handle language very easily.

Organizational Aptitudes. It is going to be very easy for you to organize and manage work groups.

Artistic Aptitudes. If you are good at drawing, creative writing or interpretation, for example.

Operational Aptitudes. Machine operation, driving, technology, is your strong point.

This is a good guide to know what you're best at. Curiously, your aptitudes will coincide with your hobbies or with the profession you have always dreamed of. It's a mental process that's easy to explain. Generally, the tasks that we find difficult, we do not like to do them. However, we enjoy the simple ones, and the final results are usually much better.

Therefore, we are going to focus on our main skills. That will be our base, the starting point on the road to success. We are able to give a correct and quick solution when it is simple, we see it so obvious, that it is difficult to make a mistake, so that's when our instinct works in our side, we only have to apply it intelligently. But, in order to achieve the success, we yearn for, we cannot rely simply on one category of skills that we have mentioned in our list. Let us take one example. Let us imagine that you always wanted to be a writer. To be a normal writer, having language skills will be enough. Now, if you want to be a successful writer, you must combine more than one skill. With language skills you will be able to write a text correctly, you will not have spelling mistakes, you will have vocabulary fluency. If you also have artistic skills, your creative process will be much better, you will invent more complex plots and your characters will gain their own personality, turning what you write into a much better product. Here, your instinct will lead you much faster to a successful situation. But, if you add to the cocktail intellectual skills, the whole process of researching scenarios, the time of your texts, the ability to keep learning new writing techniques that give freshness to your novels, as well as the dramatic changes provided by the study of previous successful authors, will further enrich your work. Success will be much closer than you think.

However, you don't always have all the skills you'd like to function at the highest possible level, so you need to be aware of your weaknesses and train them conscientiously, and try to balance the maximum power of your innate skills with the skills to be learned. As you get it, and without hardly perceiving it, your instinct is going to rise in the level of certainty, in the speed of response.

But man does not live by aptitudes alone. There are other factors that play a crucial role and are just as necessary to achieve our goal of economic success.

3.2.Motivation.

According to an article by *Pepe Rodríguez*, motivation is defined as the need or desire that activates and directs our behaviour (...) is the fact of activating and orienting behaviour, the force behind our craving for food, for sexual intimacy, and our desire to be able to reach them.

(...) The most important element of motivation lies in the way we feel emotionally in a given situation. A primary element is the way we feel our emotions.

(...) If motivation explains behavior and, behavior is explained by specific instincts, then motivation and instincts would be interchangeable. Instinct: complex behavior fixed through a species and that is not learned (is innate).

(in SlideShare, 23/02/2014).

The second basic factor is motivation. In order to strengthen our aptitudes, to learn to handle new ones, we need a high degree of motivation twenty-four hours a day; and not only to maintain it, but to feed it continuously.

Motivation is what drives us to do things, it is the fuel needed to move the engine of instinct. Let's set an example again. When we are thirsty, an irremediable thirst, our instinct will direct us quickly where we can find a glass of water, that instinct is motivated by thirst. That motivation to drink water is the one that leads us anxiously towards the liquid and doesn´t leave until we quench our thirst. That motivation that allows us to pull out our instinct for some necessary action, vital for us, is called intrinsic motivation, we all carry it within us.

But there is another equally important kind of motivation in the issue we are dealing with, because that is what we are going to work on so that our instincts lead us to financial freedom. The following example is very significant and important to reach our goal. Make no mistake, we work for money, we like our work and our profession more, or we like it less. Therefore, the main motivation we have to go to work is to get paid.

Obviously, if we like what we do, instinctively our motivation will be very different from if we don't like it. In the first choice, when what we do we make it motivated, the instinct will lead you to make decisions focused on getting a little more, and the whole mechanism of growth is set in motion at full speed, is the gear and chain, the instinct

feeds motivation, and motivation makes our instinct more insightful, it will make it much more potent. And there will come a time when you begin to realize that, the same work you do for others, you can do for yourself. You have a foundation to achieve it, because you have aptitudes,

you have a great motivation to move adequately the aptitudes that you have, and your instinct is already telling you that you can do more and better, is leading you as if by magic on the road to success, to your financial freedom.

If you think about it, motivation makes the effort you make to achieve your goal much greater, getting to it before the deadlines, will encourage your instinct to work much faster, often transforming it into initiative, and your ability to learn and develop other complementary skills, those that you do not possess will also grow..

Motivation is the art of not giving up. We have already said on more than one occasion that walking the road is neither easy nor fast, we are going to run into numerous obstacles, and having a maximum level of motivation will keep us strong. Here your instinct intervenes by saying don't give up, you can, nurturing your motivation. The final incentive is much more powerful than the obstacles. Being aware of it, let your instinct work.

Now we seem to have it all done. That's it, we have what we need. But no, there are still a couple more factors to explore before to meet all the optimal conditions for achieving our financial independence on the basis of our instinct.

3.3. Preparation.

Instinct is useless, or having motivation at its best, if we are not prepared. You can have great ideas without knowing how to carry them out. So, the first impulse of our instinct must be to prepare ourselves properly in the discipline in which we want to succeed, and consequently, to enjoy financial freedom.

ἓν οἶδα ὅτι οὐδὲν οἶδα. I just know I don't know anything. We start from scratch, questioning everything we think we know, and consider learning as much as we can. Don't be afraid, leave your prejudices aside and start preparing yourself. You are developing your instinct, trust it and start making small decisions on the basis of him. Preparation is neither more nor less than the training of your aptitudes.

We'll go back to one of the old assumptions. You want to be a writer, you know or have discovered your good expression and use of language, you are creative, and it is easy to write texts. Your family members usually commission you to dedicate anniversaries, speeches at weddings, because they know you're doing well.

It's a start. The next door to opening wide on your way to success is to train those qualities. And we don't mean putting on and writing ten hours a day. No, that will come later. First you must read to others. There is nothing more educational than learning from someone who was previously successful. Read and take notes, look at the structures, at the vocabulary, untangle the characters, study all the complexity of many great works. Then, take a course in microreporting, then a course in short stories. And practice what you learn. Don't worry, you have skills and motivation, you are preparing, your instinct is very difficult to fail. Keep training always as if it was the first day, your body, as you master the discipline trained, you will ask for more.

The freedom in finance is going to be given to you by the fact that you don't need the help you used to need in order to reach the final objective. On the contrary, the more you need you, the

freer you'll be. The effect is like an avalanche. It starts as a small snowball, nobody notices its existence, and rolling cautiously, you end up being a tremendous unstoppable avalanche.

But never forget where you came from, don't forget that you started out as a tiny snowflake. That will motivate you even more, that humility will keep your instinct alert, your good judgment and you will always have a greater objective to fulfill.

Paolo Maldini was one of the best football players in history in his defensive position. He made his AC Milan debut at the age of 17 and retired at 41, when normally a defending professional football player retires with a maximum of 36 or 37. He spent his entire career in the same team in which he made his debut, winning every possible AC Milan trophy, both collective and personal. With his team, he played a final of a world championship and another final of a European championship. He had a voracious instinct, extraordinary physical and technical skills, but never stopped training them, so he was able to retire so late playing at such a high level, had the humility of the same boy who made his debut in 1985, when he did in 2009. *Maldini*'s business was football, he discovered his skills and was always motivated above others, he prepared and did not fail to do so throughout his sporting career. *Paolo Maldini* was the best paid defender of his time, his financial freedom did not come from birth, he earned it himself. His instinct was decisive, but not only his instinct, his aptitudes or his preparation. The last essential element to reach the top, constancy.

3.4. Constancy.

Perseverance is neither more nor less than perseverance in the pursuit of our goal. Your instinct will tell you what decision to make, it will be splendidly decisive, that is why

it is so important to have it activated, motivated and trained, but if you are not constant, you will be the flower of a day. Consistency is the daily work, it is to put into practice all the writing courses that your instinct advised you to do, and how motivated you completed them. The constancy is *Paolo Maldini* going to the training every day without fainting.

Today modern life constantly tempts us with a rosary of comforts, an enormous number of tools that provide absolutely everything, although most of the time we do not realize it. We have accommodated ourselves to think that we are making a great effort to achieve all the objectives we have set ourselves, without knowing if, really, we are being constant or not in that effort.

To be constant is not only to go to work, it is also not to give up when things come badly given, it is to face the possibility of failure with the strength and strength enough to overcome it, if one day you do not get things as you had planned. And for that you need to be really motivated, prepared and totally sure that, whatever the cost, you will reach your goal. Working for days, months or years in search of a goal that does not motivate us at all, is a real torture, as well as a waste of time.

Constancy and discipline are first cousins. The most illustrative example we can give to define constancy or inconstancy is that of the gym. In the gym there are times when there is no one who can catch a free machine and others in which only the faithful go to the exercise, the really constant.

Many people pay for the annual offers offered by the gyms because they are cheap compared to the monthly ones, but they only go after Christmas, a couple of weeks, at most a month, for the purposes of New Year's Eve, just before the summer holidays, a few times to try to show off a nice body on the beach; and just after those summer holidays, to try to take off the fattened kilos. The statistic of constancy in the gym tells us that half of the people who sign up for the gym leave before they are six months old.

"With constancy and tenacity, you get what you want; the word impossible has no meaning."

(Napoleón)

To get the annual bonus is the simple thing, and to do the story of the milkmaid thinking that in four sessions you are going to be at maximum is only a dream, and not to try to think in the medium or long term. For the most part, they are unable to adapt to the routine of frequent sessions. Others get bored because they don't really like it, many more, after all day working, get lazy going to crush

themselves. If they don't succeed quickly, they give up, they are not constant. The really important thing when it comes to going to the gym is to be motivated, to be constant and to like doing that sport.

Setting short term objectives is totally licit, interesting and recommendable, but they must be objectives that can be met in that short space of time, to progress little by little, that will help you stay motivated. But it is one thing to win one battle, two battles, and quite another to win the war.

That mission is always going to be a long-term goal, it will be an important goal, and also necessary, you can´t live on small goals, you can get stuck in them, and in the long run can also lead to failure.

"The one who has moved the mountain is the one who began by removing the small stones."

(Chinese Proverb)

4. The arrival of Success. How to manage it.

"Success in a man's life is in preparing to seize the occasion when it presents itself."

Benjamin Disraeli

We can add to this famous phrase of *Disraeli* that, to arrive before anyone else to achieve that success in life,

the factor that differentiates one from the other is the instinct they need to see that they are being presented with that occasion.

Throughout this book, we have given some guidelines to follow so that our instinct is properly prepared to get where others do not arrive or arrive before others. All the factors we need to work on so that our instinct is bold, fast, effective and decisive in the right decisions we make in a working day, and that our work is valued enough to make us financially independent. It does not mean that our financial freedom is equivalent to freedom to work. Not everyone is ready to work on their own, who has an aptitude for it, or motivates him to work for himself. Yes, we all work for ourselves, after all, but it can be done within a team environment, with supervisors and managers setting the goals for us, but it is important that they have full confidence in our instinct for those goals to be achieved.

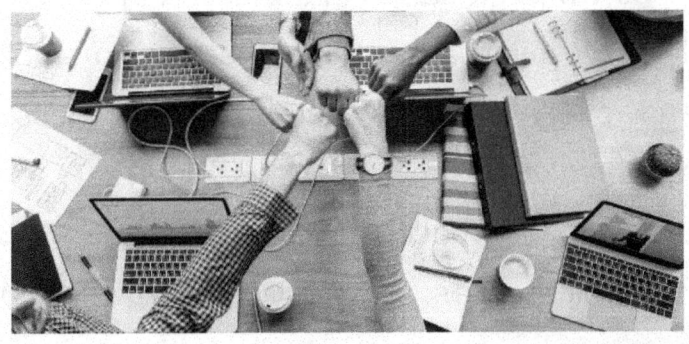

Once we have opened all the doors that lead to financial success, when we have reached the end of the road, we must know how to manage it, something like not swimming to die on the shore. If we don't know how to handle it, we can just as easily leave.

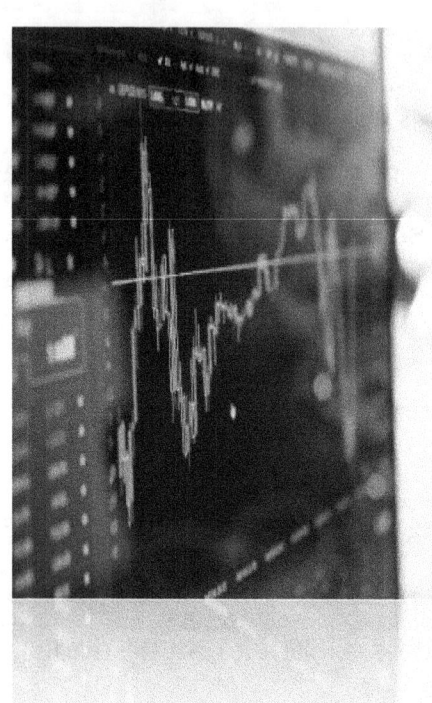

You can't just enjoy success. Many times, success comes so early that we are not mature enough to carry it on our shoulders. The best recipe for managing success, as we put it earlier in the case of Paolo Maldini, is humility. We must accept that there is no small goal, each and every one of the financial successes we achieve will make us grow. We must always try to give a little more each day, because that is what will allow us to mark the differences. Personal satisfaction is an individual triumph, no matter how much you work as a team.

A humble person and, in turn, with a predator instinct to achieve success, will always be much better recognized than someone paid for himself. Humility will open many doors. The subjective and relative sense of success is also implicit in its very definition, and refers only to the resolution of objectives, the closeness of your personal goals or an advance in the way to reach the point you've outlined each day, everything will depend on your skills and the motivation with which you perform the tasks. Success depends

fundamentally on the constancy with which the person who tries to achieve an objective, employs on it. It is essential that those who try to succeed in the adventure of financial independence, are able to have high expectations and desire to fight for their goal, success can´t be related to idleness, laziness or negativism. Success should not be treated as a single-sided coin, but as the attainment of an objective, the arrival at the end of the road, be it small and personal, only as self-satisfaction, or much larger and with great impact.

It is important to reflect that the achievement of a certain success is also accompanied by an increase in responsibility, and that many times it can give us vertigo just before achieving it, come down and fail at the last moment, something like the stage fright referred to by *Jorge Valdano*.

Frances Vaughan (n.d.) quoted by (*Roosman*, 2011) says: "Intuition allows us to resort to the enormous supply of knowledge of which we are not aware, including not only all that one has intentionally or subliminally experienced or learned, but also the infinite reservoir of universal knowledge, in which the limits of the individual are surpassed."

Executives do a lot of things in addition to making decisions. But only executives make decisions. Therefore, the first managerial attitude is to make effective decisions. (*Drucker*, 1989).

ARH is undergoing great changes and innovations, especially now that we are on the threshold of the third millennium... In this new context, the people are no longer the problem of organizations, but the solution to their problems. People cease to be the challenge to become the competitive advantage of organizations that know how to deal with them; people cease to be the most important organizational resource to

become the main business partner. (*Chiavenato*, 2000).

In any kind of decision, whether it is a more or less important decision, there is an aspect that is never going to disappear, it is the capacity to face the risks and the uncertainty of the final results. Only those who have the best instinct to make that decision will succeed. They tend to say against intuitive decisions that are so risky and irrational, that the percentage of success cannot be high. We affirm that, if we do not trust our instinct, there will be no decision to make, so we will remain stuck in the same place forever.

But not everything is intuition, we must first analyze the situation, evaluate it calmly, and then we will use the instinct to decide the objectives and offer all possible alternatives to achieve them effectively and quickly.

"The decision is the most human of acts (because) it is the combination of the analytical faculties of observation, knowledge and intuition of human beings." (Curzio, 1998).

However, we must note that any kind of decision we make, even those derived from an objective approach previously filtered by scripts to follow, will face the problem that meditated decisions, taken as fundamental in the rational decision-making model, are less effective when a margin for irrationality is also established.

5.Conclusion.

To conclude, our personal bet for the inclusion of that margin of irrationality that instinctive decisions give us, we can base it on a statement as mundane as the one that says that the world belongs to the brave. Decision-making based on

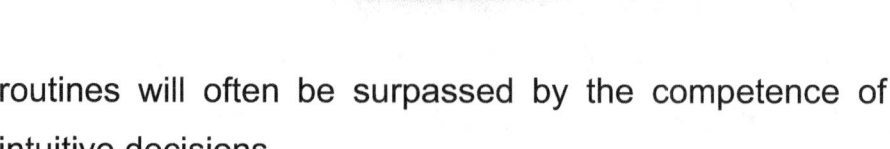

routines will often be surpassed by the competence of intuitive decisions.

Intuition is a way of knowing reality and judging whether a course of action is appropriate or not. Intuitive judgments are quick, unconscious, involuntary, and emotionally charged, in the sense that the one who intuits a thing is somehow committed to what he intuits. Intuition does not know how to give reasons why it believes what it intuits. If it knew how to give them, it would no longer be intuition, it would be reasoning. In a certain sense intuition and reasoning are two different ways of judging a situation.

Intuition as an experienced judgment is the intuition of an expert in a matter, who just by observing what is happening takes charge of the situation and knows how to act. This is the case of the experienced doctor, who just by looking at the patient and with a couple of questions already knows what is happening to him.

It's an expert's judgment. Intuition as an experienced judgment has many possibilities of being valid. It all depends on how expert it is who makes the judgment. It comes from an accumulated and implicit knowledge that one has, which allows one to save reasoning.

(Miguel Ángel Ariño. La toma de Decisiones).

THE ENTERPRISING WOMAN TODAY

INDEX.

Chapter 1. The role of working women in today's society.

Chapter 2. Qualities of the enterprising woman.

Chapter 3. Advice on becoming an entrepreneur.

Chapter 4. How to build an influential business.

Chapter 5. The great entrepreneurial women of the 21st century.

Chapter 1.

The role of working women in today's society.

Not many years ago, maybe a couple of decades ago, three at most, a high percentage of women were exclusively engaged in housework. Taking care of the children, keeping the house clean, making food. The work of a housewife is probably the hardest in the world, but it has its great advantages which, although it looks like it won't, will be important.

Until recently, mothers have raised their daughters be housewives. They continue to do so, regardless of whether the mentality has changed, the management of the home is led by women. The transformation is progressive. From simple housewives, they became both housewives and part-time workers.

Later, with the same evolution of society, which becomes fiercely consumerist, it is necessary that two salaries enter the family nucleus. It is normal, of the basic necessities, now it is not enough to have food and basic electrical appliances, also the leisure requires money to reach a status of life with a minimum of quality. Nowadays it is rare where there is not more than one television at home, computer, Smartphone for each member of the family, to give an example.

So the full-time incorporation of women into the world of work is a fact. Nevertheless, they are still, a

nd rightly so, the commanders of domestic life. Although

the man begins to carry out the tasks of a housewife, it is only a help with all the burden of managing the home.

And we come to the last "link" in the evolution of women's work. Above all, since the second decade of this century, women have made the final leap. Now, many women run companies by themselves, occupy high positions in the most important and profitable firms around the world, are a high percentage of total entrepreneurship, and, moreover, are still mothers, wives and housewives.

In fact, if we stop to think about it, women are much more prepared than men. Since they are girls, their mothers have already taught them, in whatever way, that they are the bosses, that they must learn to manage and command, and that they must do it well.

So the base is almost innate, so the process of becoming an enterprising woman has already begun. But you must know that it is not to arrive and become a successful entrepreneur overnight. Being an entrepreneur takes a whole process that you need to go through.

With this book, we are going to advise you how to do it, what qualities you must have and, if you don't have them, or think you don't have them, how to discover them, acquire them or enhance them, the steps you must follow to reach the goal. We are going to give you a potentially successful business model, how to create it, the bases it must have.

And finally, we're going to show you examples of women entrepreneurs who, not only have been successful as entrepreneurs, but you can also find them in the Forbes list of the richest people in the world. They are examples to follow and, who knows, you may also become one of those who make up that list.

Chapter 2.

Qualities of the enterprising woman.

The first thing we are going to do is to describe to you what qualities you must have to become an enterprising woman. Thus, you yourself will be able to discover which of them you have, which you have, but you must strengthen, and which you must acquire

for a complete preparation.

The first quality we must attend to is **talent**. The definition of talent is associated with innate aptitude or intelligence coefficient. It is the ability we have to exercise a profession or to do any job. Talent is associated with innate ability and the creativity that comes with that aptitude, although it can also be enhanced or acquired through practice and training.

Talent is often explained as the manifestation of emotional intelligence, which is knowing how to recognize and lead your feelings, towards motivation and management of social relationships.

Innate or inherited talent never disappears, it is part of you, although it can be enhanced with training, practice and continuous learning. The acquired talent, on the other hand, must be learned and trained in a perennial way.

Acquiring certain skills is quite simple, it is important to know the skills you have, and complement them with other compatible talents. Some, you can learn, others, with simple experience are acquired.

In the business world, talent and instinctive workers are becoming more and more important. The system is to discover in what kind of work the worker feels more at ease, does the tasks before, and also enjoys them, because the end result is a much higher return, which is to the benefit of both the company and the worker. The figure of the coach, an expert in work psychology, who knows the methods to get the best out of you, will help you discover what talents you possess.

The second quality that an enterprising woman must have is the product of the first. Your talent will lead you irremediably to **Inspiration**. To make it better understood, let's give an example. If your main talent is interpreting, you can work on it by doing specific courses in interpretative techniques, you can attend actresses' seminars, in which they tell you about their methods of concentration, their breathing technique, how they face a text to create the character they must interpret, how to relax before the nerves of the premiere.

All this is valid and complementary. But the truth is that, when the moment of truth arrives, you will be alone on the stage in front of the audience. If you have the talent to be an actress, inspiration is the weapon that will detonate a sublime performance, above all other actresses.

Inspiration is closely anchored to the spontaneous stimulus that arises inside an artist or when creating. Inspiration does not appear by effort or will; therefore, it cannot be trained or developed by force of will. Inspiration is there and appears when talent calls it.

However, no matter how much talent you have to develop a business, and no matter how much inspiration your talent gives you, you're not going to make it without a good dose of **perseverance** and **constancy**. It's all very well for you to be very clear about what's best for you, to have great ideas, but you have to work and be constant.

Nothing comes without effort. Perseverance is not giving up for many obstacles that are put in front of you, is to overcome that desire to surrender when you fail again, again, again. Do not despair, if the work you develop, if the company you have created has a solid foundation, in the end the results will come.

Perseverance in your idea imprints character, a kind of inner invincibility. And women, as a general rule, possess that much more developed quality than men, for a simple reason: women have always had very difficult to achieve the entrepreneurial success of men, and not because they are not the same or more prepared than they are, but because the ecosystem of men in business has functioned in this way by decree for centuries. Now, that ecosystem is seriously threatened, and they put many impediments on a woman to get to the top of that pyramid.

The woman has always had to fight double or triple to get allowed to get the half they allow a man, financially speaking. And that is perhaps why perseverance, constancy, strength of character, is much more developed than in most men.

The last of the qualities we must point out is **openness of mind**. Once you have your business up and running, you should not think that you are the only one who knows how best to run the business. If you have a professional team at your service, each doing what they do best, they are quite likely to be better than you in those areas where you have delegated roles. It denotes intelligence that way of surrounding yourself.

That team, if it works on what it knows how to do, and with a certain margin of freedom, the people who make it up, squeezing their talents, will work happily, and they themselves will worry about looking for ways for your initial idea to continue growing. Having an open mind to these new ideas is going to be very important, because the business will be continually renewed, it will have its own personality.

Be careful, having an open mind does not mean giving up or delegating decision making, it means listening to what those who work for you have to say, and being able to create better business strategies, new alternatives, to make the best decisions, and constantly renew your success.

Chapter 3.

Advice on becoming an entrepreneur.

Once we've talked about the qualities you should have when starting your business venture, it's time to get going. To do this, we have devised a series of tips that will help you consider how you should function as an entrepreneur.

The first thing we want to advise you is to be prudent with

your ideas. It won't do you any good airing what you want to do. Do it, work it, the result is that this work will speak for itself., people will tell that you´re an entrepreneur, you won´t need to publish it by yourself.

If you're willing to start your business idea, you should take it seriously. You have to put all your senses in the elaboration of your project. Draw up your plans, put yourself, in principle, short and simple goals to achieve.

This will motivate you and help you move forward. But whatever you do, always 100%.

When you know your talent, you are ready to develop it to the maximum, make sure that the company you are going to open is related to something that, in addition, you are passionate about. Think that your work strategy, your dreams, your hopes and your goals, you are going to deposit them there, as someone who invests his most precious treasure so that it multiplies. This way of thinking will make your day to day a new adventure, a new way to grow, no matter if you are going to earn more or less money today.

Think that, even if you undertake to earn money, this is only the result of your work, that the goals you are setting are the most important, the more you grow your goals, the result will come alone, you will not have to worry

about it.

Develop communication with the outside world, your social skills, advertise your work. Yes, your job, not your person. Think that the best way to advertise is for your work to speak for itself, to be excellent, serious, developed. This will make it much easier to expand. Obviously, you are the visible head of your company, so, if you know how to reach people with your work, people, through it, will reach you.

Take a chance. Taking risks doesn't mean throwing yourself into the void. Your mind is full of ideas, develop them, create a work plan, with alternatives, with the

possibilities of success that you can have if you make one decision or take others. These are measured risks. Nevertheless, you know that you have talent, that you have developed that talent with studies, with previous experience, with a lot of work, but thanks to that you also have developed the instinct. Trust your instinct, your inspiration, because those instinctive decisions give rise to the greatest successes. That's why taking risks from time to time is necessary and healthy.

Never, absolutely never, ever be afraid of failure. Whoever fears failure is condemned to live with it for life and will never get anywhere. There will always be people who will criticize your way of doing things, but you are sure of what you are doing, and nothing and no one can stop you. Therein lies one of the secrets of your future success.

Naturally, not all your decisions or moves are going to be right, no one is infallible, but use those little failures to learn from them. If you use your mistakes in a positive way, you may make mistakes in other decisions, but in those mistakes you will not fall again.

Analyze your mistakes, discover the causes and find a remedy, look for other solutions to the problems you are going to face every day. Therein lies your strength, in perseverance despite losing small battles, because your goal is, in the end, to win the war.

Preach by example, that your employees see that you are the first to arrive at work, that you are the last to leave, that you are really looking for success in your business. Think of yourself as the boss, and that's precisely why you should be the best employee you have. It will also have an impact on the performance of others.

An important tip for the development of your idea is to surround yourself with a good work team. To do this, explore what your weak points are and hire someone who, those less strong points, are part of their skills. Having people with you trained in aspects of the business that you don't master but that are necessary will give your project an extra edge. Listen to their advice and make decisions based on them. A company is not just one person, and having the right team is synonymous with victory. That way, you can reach your goal sooner and better.

It is also important that this team believes in you, that they think your project is good and that, with you at the forefront, everything that is projected will come to fruition. That question will also motivate them.

Finally, don't stop investigating. Constantly recycle your skills and try to acquire new knowledge. What today is synonymous with success, tomorrow is going to be obsolete. Therefore, work in innovation, you must be up to date with all the advances you can bring, new ideas, new techniques, new work strategies. Give them your personal touch and be creative with it. Try to do the same, but in a way that only you do.

Chapter 4.

How to build an influential business.

You're ready to start, but you may not know how or in what to do it. We are going to propose a series of actions to develop in order to start working and create an influential business model.

When you start a business, the first thing you need is money. So you have to work out a small project. Knowing what your talent is, think about what you'd like to do, develop a plan with objectives and the tools you'll need.

On top of that, make a first expense budget.

With the complete dossier of your small project, go to the help centre for entrepreneurial women that each municipality has. There, they will help you get started. They will advise you on the financial aid you have, what is the best way to start, and they will adjust the budget. They are experts and work with it on a daily basis.

Explain your work philosophy, once you have the elements to start, the best way to make your company known can be in any forum in the field in which you are going to undertake. Say what you want them to know about your brand, how you are going to develop it, sell your idea.

Regardless of whether your business presence is physical, create a virtual one as well. Working with the network, nowadays, is essential. And we don't mean that your company is going to be online, no, we mean that you use the net to promote it. There are professionals dedicated exclusively to positioning you. This aspect will be valuable when your business is known and influential.

The decisions you make about your company must follow a script, a clear objective. Your strategic decisions depend on that script, they will become the leitmotiv of your company. If you create a good work philosophy, according to the philosophy that your clients are going to look for in you, they will trust it and they will look for you. This is what we call empathy with the client. Look for and find the age ranges of your potential customers, their economic status, anything that can help you get close to them, and focus your goals on them.

Always think about your customers, do not try to sell for sell, whether your professional services or the products you offer, rather help them. Offer yourself as a guide and accompany them in their search. If you know how to do it, you can be sure that your success is assured.

Trace a small market field to begin with, something you can control yourself with no problem or need for anyone else. Short and possible goals. From there, expand as your business becomes more and more influential.

Hire someone only when you need to. We have to remind you that the principle is always difficult, there are always decisions that are going to fail you and you must learn from them. The sooner you get the experience, you will see that everything is flowing as you had thought.

Elaborate, create or apply an influential strategy to improve your business MLM is an innovative method that every entrepreneur should consider, because this is where you as an entrepreneur should focus your marketing efforts, so that your group of affiliates and leaders are the key bearers when it comes to influencing potential customers.

This influential marketing strategy accompanied by online reviews, blogs, opinions expressed through discussion forums, media information, and social exchange, are the online communities that play a key role in influencing decisions when affiliating a prospect.

So, instead of having your influential strategy target a large audience, you should target influential people (affiliates and leaders), so that they deliver the message of your brand, product or service to the desired audience.(...)

Identifying relevant influencing factors.

Researching who your target audience is and how they are connected to you.

Preparing the development of your strategy.

Aligning the strategy with your business goals and objectives.

Making a commitment through the content you share with your followers.

Participating with your followers in an authentic way, being real from the beginning, not being so would end up with a relationship that can be long lasting.

Using paid social media, to amplify your content.

Finally collecting data, measuring adjustments and optimizing your campaign.

Remember, influential marketing is not easy, and should not be rushed. Be organized build a good strategy by spending time on research.

Don't think it works for everyone, adapt your approach to each influencing factor in a specific way.

Be patient, and always remember that influence is not equal to your popularity. After all, what you are looking for is a specific customer action, not a specific scope.

Once you apply this method to influence your affiliates and leaders with this new strategy, rest assured that in a short period of time you will have improved the marketing of your MLM business.

(Quote: *Osvaldo Polar* "*Elaborar una estrategia Influyente*")

Chapter 5.

The great entrepreneurial women of the 21st century.

Oprah Winfrey's story is one of the best examples of entrepreneurship. Her life, has been a constant work of improvement.

Oprah Winfrey is a speaker, actress, writer and producer, best known for her work on her own television show, *The*

Oprah Winfrey Show. *Oprah*'s show aired for twenty-five seasons, from 1986 to 2001.

Oprah Gail Winfrey was born on January 29, 1954 in Kosciusko, a rural town in Mississippi. She spent the first six years of her life on her maternal grandmother's farm in Mississippi. She then moved with her mother to a poor neighborhood in Milwaukee, Wisconsin.

When she was nine years old, she was raped by one of her cousins. The teenager began the series of sexual abuses, *Winfrey* suffered over the next five years at the hands of three other men, all "friends" of the family.

When she was a teenager, the rebellion nearly led her to a reformatory. She was not sent to a detention center because she moved in with her father, a barber from Nashville. Under her parent's care, she went from delinquent to honor roll, won Miss Black America and was chosen as Nashville High School's most popular student, and won an oratorical scholarship to Tennessee State University in 1971.

"I feel that luck happens when preparation meets opportunity."

At the age of nineteen, she became the first African American woman to appear on a Nashville newscast because she got a job as an announcer for a local television network.

In 1976, she moved to Baltimore, Maryland and worked as a presenter for *"People Are Talking"*. There she discovered that this was not the ideal line of work for her because she couldn't help crying when she had to tell sad news.

In Illinois, seven years later, she visualized where to go with her career. She went from working on the AM Chicago show to running her own show, *"The Oprah Winfrey Show"*. In the first half of the 1980s he met *Stedman Graham*, with whom he still has a relationship.

In September 1985, *"The Oprah Winfrey Show"* began broadcasting nationwide. The program was presented on 120 channels and had an audience of 10 million people. By the end of the first year, it had defeated *"The Phil Donahue Show"* (the first television show with interviews) and raised one hundred and twenty-five million, thirty of which made up *Winfrey*'s salary.

In the same year, she won a role in the film "*The Color Purple*", directed by *Steven Spielberg,* and was nominated for an Oscar for Best Supporting Actress. The previous one was her first work as an actress, but not her last. Among her other roles is the one she played in the 1998 film *"Beloved"*, based on Toni Morrison's Pulitzer-winning novel.

Shortly thereafter, she gained full control of the program by including it under the control of the production company she herself created, Harpo Productions. As a result, the program's audience continued to grow.

In 1994 most talk shows sought to explore vulgar and sensational themes, but *Oprah Winfrey* decided not to follow her competition's example. Although this initially had a negative effect on his audience level, in the long run viewers learned to appreciate the dignity with which he handled the program.

In 2009 it was announced that *Oprah Winfrey* would abandon its show once its contract with ABC ended (in 2011). After leaving the program, *Oprah* began working on its own television network, Oprah Winfrey Network.

"The only good thing about economic success is that it gives you the ability to concentrate on the things that really matter. And that means making a difference, not only in your own life, but above all in the lives of others."

In 2003, she became the first African American woman to join Forbes magazine's list of billionaires.

She is actively involved with several charitable organizations, including: Oprah's Angel Network, which supports and promotes the creation of other charitable organizations and has raised more than fifty-one million for this purpose; A Better Chance, which provides scholarships for students of color; and Family for Better Lives, an organization that brings education and medicine to places where it is needed such as Uttarakhand (in northern India) and Yonibana (West Africa).

In November 2013, she was honored with the Presidential Medal of Freedom, an award given to her by President *Barack Obama* that is considered the highest decoration a civilian in the United States can have access to.

(Source: www.historia-biografia.com)

Our next star is another woman who knew how to exploit her talent to the maximum and is one of the references of entrepreneurial woman of worldwide success.

Carolina Herrera is an American Venezuelan fashion designer, known for her elegance and class to dress celebrities around the world. Born into a rich family and coming from a privileged world, her mother instilled in her passion and discipline that helped transform her into an elegant woman. During the seventies and eighties, she was well known in Venezuela for the fact that she was considered one of the best dressed women in the country.

Later, the family moved to New York where she decided to become a fashion designer. Despite not having any training as a designer she soon became very successful with her designs and was wearing some of the most famous women in the world, which led to a huge boom in the popularity of her clothes.

Since then, she has continued to expand her line of luxury products in the 1980s, including perfume, Cologne, wedding dresses, handkerchiefs, handbags and other accessories. His company has become one of the most successful fashion houses in New York. Her skills as a designer are so recognized that she has won numerous awards for her work. She has been able to build a brand that is very distinguished and respected in the world of haute couture.

(Source: www.thefamouspeople.com)

Our last example of an enterprising woman, overcoming all kinds of obstacles despite her preparation, is that of the Greek journalist *Arianna Huffington.*

Arianna Huffington, writer and columnist, and co-founder of the prestigious digital magazine *"The Huffington Post"*, could say emphatically that she has not wasted a second of her 62 years. His drive and talent must have run in his family, as his father *Konstantinos* was a dream journalist who published in underground newspapers during the German occupation of Greece. This led him straight to the concentration camps, where he spent the rest of the war and where he happened to meet *Arianna*'s mother.

His exciting career began at the age of 16 when he moved to England to study Economics at Girton College in Cambridge. Five years later, she became president of the Cambridge Union Society, a prestigious debating community that in its almost two centuries of existence had only been presided over by two women.

A few years later, she begins to be known for her conservative stance against feminism, and she states this in the first of her thirteen books, *"The Female Woman"* (1973), in which she writes:

"The frenetic extremism of the women's liberation movement is not seeking the emancipation of women, but the destruction of society."

In 1986 he formalized his relationship with *Michael Huffington,* heir to the Texas oil and gas industry and Republican candidate for the U.S. Congress, passing through the altar and later having two daughters. Eleven years later, his marriage ends and since then he has been chased by a few love and labor scandals: in 1998, *Michael Huffington* publicly revealed that he was bisexual and has also received numerous plagiarism accusations for the biographies he wrote, including *Maria Callas*.

After writing great biographies and developing her columnist facet, with the new century, the writer sweeps away a renewed mentality much more liberal and vindictive facing causes such as the intervention of the United States in Yugoslavia, the fight for the manufacture of greener cars and even independently run for governor of California, which ended up winning *Schwarzenegger*.

But all this was just the preparation of the ground for what

was really going to take his feet off the ground. In 2005, *Arianna* created *"Huffingtonpost.com",* a blog portal that modestly invited experts in different areas to upload original, quality content. In 2006, it was included in the list of the most influential people in the world. The platform started with 500 bloggers and today has more than six thousand, and records 500 million pages views per month.

In April 2015, *"The Huffington Post"* wins the first Pulitzer Prize in the category of National Journalism, thanks to journalist *David Wood,* one of the 125 full-time members of the newspaper's team.

Arianna is a clear example of how important it is not only to be in the right place at the right time, but also how valuable it is to have vision, dreams, ambitions and work motivations. He rode the big wave of digital journalism, and a few years later the most reputable and successful independent magazine was bought by the giant AOL for 231.4 million euros.

A flesh-and-blood fighter who will surely be able to look back very proudly and who begins to look forward with a much calmer vision of reality: she spends more and more time with her daughters in New York and, as she said in one of the talks in the last TED Woman,

"The way to a more productive, inspiring and happy life is to get enough sleep every day,"

he pointed out. With that trajectory, everyone could sleep peacefully.

(Source: www.codigonuevo.com)

We have chosen the model of these three women specifically for one reason: *Oprah Winfrie* has its origins in an unstructured family, comes from the most absolute poverty, and has reached the top from scratch.

Arianne Huffington was born into a middle-class family, having the opportunity to train herself by developing her talent to exploit it to the fullest, overcoming the obstacles she encountered along the way without fainting.

Carolina Herrera was born and raised in a rich family. Even so, having everything at hand, she decided to seize the reins of her destiny by making herself, getting everything for the value of her work.

Some had some tools, another, however, had different ways. All of them have made the most of their work as entrepreneurs, from their intelligence and preparation.

Take into account the advice we have given you in this book, exploit your talent, do not falter, enjoy what you do and draw up a good plan that will lead you to the goal you want to propose, either financial or work realization. Your instinct is going to tell you where and when you are going to put the opportunity to undertake for yourself.

It's a good tactic to look at how these women, and many others, have achieved their goals, and adapt them to your dreams, to your day-to-day life.

By this we mean that it doesn't matter where you come from, don't look at the obstacles you have but the opportunities to achieve success with the tools you have, because if you set your mind to it, the world is in your hands.

www.ingramcontent.com/pod-product-compliance
Lightning Source LLC
Chambersburg PA
CBHW072200170526
45158CB00004BB/1718